How to Find Your Focus, Overcome Your ADHD Symptoms and Live a Better Life

Sara Elliott Price

Published in The USA by:
Success Life Publishing
125 Thomas Burke Dr.
Hillsborough, NC 27278

Copyright © 2015 by Sara Elliott Price

ISBN-10: 1511740973

ALL RIGHTS RESERVED. No part of this publication may be reproduced or transmitted in any form whatsoever, electronic, or mechanical, including photocopying, recording, or by any informational storage or retrieval system without the express written permission from the author, except for the use of brief quotations in a book review.

Disclaimer

Every effort has been made to accurately represent this book and its potential. Results vary with every individual, and your results may or may not be different from those depicted. No promises, guarantees or warranties, whether stated or implied, have been made that you will produce any specific result from this book. Your efforts are individual and unique, and may vary from those shown. Your success depends on your efforts, background and motivation.

The material in this publication is provided for educational and informational purposes only and is not intended as medical advice. The information contained in this book should not be used to diagnose or treat any illness, metabolic disorder, disease or health problem. Always consult your physician or health care provider before beginning any nutrition or exercise program. Use of the programs, advice, and information contained in this book is at the sole choice and risk of the reader.

Table of Contents

Introduction 1

Chapter 1: Back to Basics 3

Chapter 2: Do I have ADHD? 8

Chapter 3: Help is at Hand 13

Chapter 4: Join the Medication Debate 18

Chapter 5: New Life, New Lifestyle 24

Chapter 6: ADHD in the Workplace 30

Chapter 7: Relationships – It Takes Two 36

Chapter 8: More Tips and Strategies 42

Conclusion 47

Introduction

Ever wonder if you might have ADHD? Maybe you're concerned about your focus, memory or behavior. Or have you been diagnosed but find it difficult to cope with the condition? Either way, this book can help.

People with ADHD have problems concentrating and remembering things. It can lead to all kinds of issues both at home and in the workplace, and those around you may lose patience or misunderstand your difficulties. In our busy lives someone who keeps slipping up or who fails to impress can find it hard to hold down a job or make any relationship work.

If you know, or suspect, you have ADHD, you're not alone. Thousands of other people are struggling too in a world that favors the smart, focused and dedicated. Your lack of attention and the fact you get easily distracted can hold you back. So what's to be done? Is it possible to overcome ADHD? Is medication the only option? How can you learn to cope?

This book will answer your questions about ADHD in adults. It will talk you through the signs and symptoms, diagnosis and treatment options. More than that – it will offer practical strategies and simple lifestyle changes that can make a real difference to how you manage your condition.

As ADHD makes it hard to concentrate for long, at the end of every chapter we'll summarize the main points. That way you can easily refer back and refresh your memory if you need to.

Chapter 1: Back to Basics

If you're reading this book, chances are you're wondering whether you have ADHD. Or maybe you've just been diagnosed with it. You may even have known for some time that you have ADHD, but you're finding it hard to cope.

So we're going to start by taking a look at the condition, and then go on to talk about what it means in practice to have ADHD, and the ways it affects adults.

What is ADHD?

ADHD is a psychiatric condition that affects your thinking and behavior. It stands for Attention-Deficit Hyperactivity Disorder. A bit of a mouthful – no wonder it's called by a bunch of initials! In other words, it's a lack of concentration that's often combined with high energy and impulsive behavior.

Before going any further, let's break down that long name and take a quick look at each word:

Attention: Focus or concentration, as in "pay attention."

Deficit: Something that's missing, like a deficit of funds.

Hyperactivity: Highly energetic, restless, can't keep still.

Disorder: A condition where the brain's normal functions are disrupted.

So the full name means that when someone has ADHD something in their brain makes it hard to focus for long, and this is often combined with restless, energetic behavior and spur-of-the-moment decisions.

ADHD is sometimes known as ADD, Attention-Deficit Disorder. Why the two names? Well, people without the hyperactivity part were first thought to have a separate condition. Then in 2013 the American Psychiatric Association reclassified the two as one disorder with some variations. You can sometimes see it written as ADD/ADHD, but technically it's more correct now to just use ADHD.

If you don't feel you're hyperactive, you may still have the disorder. Not even all kids with ADHD are hyperactive, and most adults aren't either. Your doctor will still be able to tell you whether you have the condition.

Isn't it just about kids?

ADHD is well known as a childhood disorder. It calls to mind hyperactive, out-of-control kids who can't sit still for a minute and have tantrums in stores. This picture isn't totally accurate, but it can definitely be the case for some children.

Kids with ADHD are often hyperactive, but not always. They usually have trouble concentrating on anything for very long because they're easily distracted. They're forgetful, dreamy, careless and given to impulsive behavior with no sense of danger. In fact, it's their lack of fear that parents usually notice first. The other symptoms come with the territory as far as young kids are concerned!

ADHD is not so well known in adults, but if you had it as a child you most likely still have it now. It's just that grown-ups can manage their behavior better than kids, so you probably seem to be holding it together pretty well. For example, instead of being hyperactive most adults with ADHD are restless, edgy and full of nervous energy.

However, many doctors believe that ADHD in adults is much more subtle than in kids. It can be hard to spot the signs. That's why it's important to get a proper diagnosis and not just carry on as you are, especially as some of the symptoms can get confused with other conditions.

Why does adult ADHD matter?

It's vital to recognize the problems ADHD can cause for both kids and adults. In fact, the age group doesn't make all that much difference. The issues are just grown-up issues instead.

Poor concentration in kids means they have difficulty learning new skills or following their lessons at school. In adults it means they can find it hard to carry out everyday tasks and responsibilities at work and at home. They can forget important dates or deadlines and risk offending their partner or the boss once too often.

Impulsive behavior in kids means they're likely to be physically reckless and put themselves in danger. Adults are more likely to make risky decisions and not think things through. If you're an adult with ADHD, chances are you're a bad driver and have probably been involved in several road traffic accidents.

And both kids and adults can have trouble getting on with others and being organized, so their lives can be stressful, full of turmoil and pretty lonely. And that can lead to other things, like depression or substance abuse, for example.

This disorder isn't something to ignore. It's important to talk to a doctor, if you haven't already, so you can get a proper diagnosis and treatment.

Summary

1. ADHD is a disorder where the brain's normal function is disrupted.

2. Adults with ADHD have poor concentration. They are forgetful, disorganized and may make bad choices. There are often problems with relationships and maybe with holding down a job.

3. If you think you may have ADHD, it's important to see a doctor to get a formal diagnosis and begin treatment.

Chapter 2: Do I have ADHD?

In this chapter we're going to take a look at people who have never been diagnosed with ADHD but think they may have it. Maybe a friend or coworker has mentioned your behavior, or you've read something about it.

If you're disorganized, restless, impetuous, and struggle with getting things done, you could be suffering from ADHD. But of course it may be just your personality, upbringing or bad habits! Or it could be some other disorder.

So how can you tell if you have ADHD? Does it have to start in childhood, or can you develop it when you get older? And when do you make that call and ask for a diagnosis?

Let's start by running through the signs that might show you have ADHD. The website webmd.com suggests the kind of thing to look out for.

Signs of ADHD in adults

Take a look at the following symptoms that describe some of the characteristics of adults with ADHD. Any of them sound familiar? Of course, a lot of people have one or two of these character traits, so saying "Yes" to a few of these doesn't mean you necessarily have ADHD.

Problems with organization and focus:

Unmethodical. You have trouble organizing yourself to pay the bills, pick up the kids, handle assignments at work or college, or meet deadlines.

Trouble prioritizing. You find it hard deciding what's important and can waste time on trivial stuff while vital deadlines come and go.

Reckless driver. You take risks, drive too fast and don't concentrate well, so you're likely to have had problems behind the wheel. Maybe you've even lost your license.

Problems with relationships:

Bad listener. You don't take in what people say and easily forget important stuff. You miss appointments, offend people or cause misunderstandings.

Edgy. You have trouble relaxing and can be tense, oversensitive and restless.

Short fuse. You have a quick temper and can lose control over small issues – but you may get over your outbursts quickly too. You also blurt out personal comments without thinking.

Divorced/separated. You're not a great listener and often fail to honor commitments. This can lead to a lot of bad feeling, as your spouse or partner sees you as uncaring.

Problems with timekeeping:

Easily distracted. You don't get things done because your attention wanders. You easily get sidetracked by other things going on. You fail to finish on time, or even at all.

Late for everything. You tend to be late a lot of the time because of being easily sidetracked. You lose track of time and also underestimate how long a task will take.

Stall for time. You put off starting a task, especially if it needs a lot of concentration. You're often running late before you start. This can add to other problems at work or home.

Think back to your childhood

Did you recognize any of these symptoms from problems you had as a child? If you did, it makes it more likely you have ADHD – but it's still too early to know for sure.

In the next chapter we'll take a look at getting a diagnosis, and you'll see why your childhood ADHD is still important. That's because ADHD is the only psychiatric disorder that never shows for the first time in adults, unlike anxiety or depression, for example. Even if you weren't diagnosed as a child, whether you showed any symptoms of ADHD back then will be a deciding factor for the doctors.

Could it be something else?

As we've seen, some of these traits can be just part of our nature. They could also be bad habits we've gotten into, or the way we were brought up. If your parents were disorganized and late for everything, for example, you may well have grown up believing that everyone was like that.

On the other hand, some of these traits can be found in other conditions. If you're restless and edgy, it could be down to an overactive thyroid or an anxiety disorder. If you have trouble concentrating, it might be due to clinical depression.

Many people who realize their habits are holding them back in life can turn themselves around. But people with ADHD find it very hard to change without therapy.

In fact, for some people ADHD leads to other problems too. They might develop obsessive-compulsive disorder to compensate for their problems in getting organized. They may become depressed or overly anxious about their behavior and what other people may be thinking. And some go on to use alcohol or drugs to try to forget their problems. These can all mask or complicate their ADHD.

So it's hard to generalize from a list of symptoms. If you think that many points on that list sound like you, the only way to be sure is to call your doctor and ask to be assessed for ADHD.

That way you can get a proper diagnosis, begin a course of therapy and start to get your life on track.

Summary

1. People with ADHD tend to be disorganized, reckless, poor listeners, always late and have a short fuse. But some of these signs can be caused by other conditions or just be down to personality or bad habits.

2. ADHD begins in childhood – it's the only psychiatric disorder that doesn't develop in adulthood.

3. If untreated, ADHD can lead to depression, anxiety and problems with alcohol or substance abuse. But getting a firm diagnosis opens the door to therapy and support, with a chance to turn your life around.

Chapter 3: Help is at Hand

So now we've looked at some of the signs that might show you have ADHD, what should you do? Well, if you feel you have many or all of the symptoms given in the last chapter, it's time to see a doctor and get a diagnosis.

Your doctor will probably work with a psychiatrist or other mental health specialists. Remember, before they can say whether or not you have ADHD, they have to rule out other problems that look similar, like thyroid conditions, anxiety disorders and clinical depression. And of course you could have something like this as well as ADHD, so the experts need to check your symptoms carefully.

Getting a diagnosis for ADHD

You might not realize it, but there's no easy way to tell if someone has this disorder. It doesn't show up in X-rays or scans. You can't do a blood test for it. So how do doctors make a diagnosis?

Well, they will ask a load of questions about your symptoms and the problems you're experiencing. You may have a questionnaire to fill in. The medical team will also need to talk to your partner or spouse, another family member or even a friend or coworker, in order to get the full picture.

Most importantly, the doctor will ask about your childhood. That's because, as we saw in the last chapter, ADHD doesn't appear for the first time in grown-ups. You may have missed out on a diagnosis when you were a kid, but the signs were there. So the doctors will be looking for clues.

ADHD symptoms in kids are things like hyperactivity, poor concentration and impulsive behavior. The condition makes it hard for children to learn and make friends, so it affects their grades and their relationships with other people. These are the kind of things the doctors will want to know about.

How well did you do at school? What were your grades like? How did you get on with other kids? What was your behavior like at home and at school? The answers will help build up a picture to show whether you had ADHD as a child. If there's no evidence to show you had it then, you don't have it now.

Once you know for sure, you'll be in a position to start a course of therapy. Even if you're not diagnosed with ADHD, the medical team will usually be able to identify whatever condition you have and offer treatment.

Most people feel so relieved at having some answers that it's like a weight off their shoulders. It also helps friends and family who have most likely been struggling to understand what's going on.

What treatment?

Many people with ADHD take medication. For some, it works wonders; for others it's not so helpful. It's important to discuss the options with your doctor. We'll be taking a closer look at medication for ADHD in the following chapter.

There are plenty of other options apart from medication. Behavioral therapy works by setting realistic goals and helping you achieve them. Social skills courses help you learn to get on with others and improve your self-confidence in social settings. Talk therapies such as counseling or psychotherapy work through any damaging emotions like anger, shame or guilt. Many people have found these treatments are very helpful.

Treating ADHD may be a matter of trial and error at first as the medical team try to find what works best for you. In fact, the best treatment for ADHD is usually to combine several options, including medication and behavioral therapy.

Working with the medical experts

Be honest. It can feel strange at first to talk to a bunch of strangers about your feelings and struggles, but they are all professionals who are there to help you. Try to be open with them.

Stick to your treatment plan. It won't help if you only take your medication or see your therapist when you remember, so find a way (or a person!) to remind you each time.

Become an expert too. Find out all you can about ADHD and especially the way it affects you. Think about your strengths and weaknesses. Explore treatment options, the different drugs and other therapies.

Keep a journal. Make a note of your symptoms and therapies as a record of your journey. Try to include as much detail as possible, as this will help you and your medical team to see how well the treatments are working or if something needs adjusting. It will also help you see the progress you make.

Is there anything else I can do?

As well as all these therapies, people with ADHD can learn some simple strategies and lifestyle changes which can make a surprising difference. We'll be looking at some of these in Chapter 5.

Summary

1. To find out if you have ADHD, a doctor will ask questions about your behavior as a child and your school grades. That's because ADHD always starts in childhood.

2. Treatment may include medication, behavioral therapy, social skills therapy and counseling. The best plan is to combine several different treatments.

3. Arrange for someone or something to remind you about your medication or therapy appointments so you stick to your treatment plan.

4. Keep a journal and note down your symptoms, therapies and other details to help doctors find the best treatment for you.

Chapter 4: Join the Medication Debate

Most people who are diagnosed with ADHD are offered medication to help control their symptoms. But like all drugs they can have side effects, and they work better for some people than others.

In this chapter we'll be looking at the most common medications and some of the risks and benefits of taking them. This will make you better informed to discuss with your doctor which one is right for you.

ADHD drugs and their side effects

ADHD medication may be in the form of a pill, but it's not a magic one! It can help with moods, concentration and behavior, but it can't cure you because as yet there's no cure for ADHD. Instead it can ease some of the symptoms. For some people it's very effective.

Once you stop taking the tablets the symptoms will come back; that's why it's important to have other therapies at the same time which teach you how to improve your behaviors or your social skills.

Stimulants. The drugs most often used to treat adult ADHD are stimulants. It may seem kind of strange to take stimulants if you are already feeling edgy and restless, but they do help you concentrate. They work by targeting a neurotransmitter in the brain called dopamine.

Commonly used stimulant drugs are Ritalin, Adderall and Dexedrine. They may be given once a day or up to three times a day, depending on whether you have the long-acting or short-acting version of the drug. Needless to say, taking a tablet once a day is easier to remember for someone with ADHD.

Taking stimulants for any length of time can be risky, because they raise your blood pressure and heartbeat. That's why you should always be under the care of a doctor, who can prescribe the right dose for you and monitor your progress. You should also remember to take your medication regularly, and you may need help to get organized and set up a system of reminders.

Side effects. As you might expect from stimulants, common side effects include feeling restless and jumpy, having a racing heartbeat, trouble sleeping, headaches and tics. You may also experience dizziness, nausea, upset stomach, loss of appetite, mood swings, depression and irritability. Many of these will fade over time.

Unpleasant but nothing unusual there, you might think. For many people the benefits are greater than the disadvantages. But take a look at the more serious stuff: some people may suffer a personality change, so they become withdrawn and listless, or show signs of obsessive-compulsive behaviors.

Red flags for stimulant drugs. According to the website helpguide.org, you should watch out for the following symptoms and **call your doctor right away** if you spot any of them. You could also tell your family and friends what to do if they notice you have any of these.

Physical symptoms:

Chest pain

Shortness of breath

Fainting

Psychiatric (mental) symptoms:

Hallucinations (seeing or hearing things that aren't real)

Paranoia (believing untrue things about other people or yourself)

Doctors have to be pretty careful when they prescribe this kind of medication. Because of these risks, stimulant drugs aren't suitable for people with certain medical complaints. These include any kind of heart problem, high blood pressure, overactive thyroid, glaucoma, psychiatric disorders, anxiety disorder and (because of the dangers if someone misuses this kind of medication) a history of drug abuse.

Non-stimulant drugs. If you can't take stimulant medication you will probably be offered an alternative, such as Strattera. Instead of targeting dopamine in the brain, these non-stimulant drugs work by raising levels of a chemical called norepinephrine.

The main advantages are that they are longer-lasting than the stimulants and work a bit like antidepressants, which is great for people with depression or anxiety issues. The disadvantage is that they're not so good at controlling restless, edgy behavior.

Strattera has similar side effects to the stimulant drugs: headaches, abdominal pain or upset stomach, dizziness and mood swings. It may also cause nausea and sleepiness.

Red flags for Strattera: Strattera has been linked to suicidal thoughts in some cases. If you feel more agitated than usual or begin to have thoughts of harming yourself, tell someone. You should also speak to a medical professional without delay. Warn your family and friends about this possible side effect and ask them to watch out for changes in your behavior.

When stimulant drugs and Strattera are not an option, your doctor may suggest treating you with antidepressants or blood pressure medication. These drugs are sometimes used to treat ADHD when nothing else is suitable.

What to ask your doctor

Now we've looked at some of the drugs and their side effects, you may be wondering if it's such a great idea to take them. Here are some questions you could ask your doctor.

Is medication right for me?

Can my symptoms be managed without medication?

What medication do you recommend for me?

How effective is it likely to be?

What are the side effects?

How long will I have to take it?

What other treatment is available?

As we mentioned before, medication works best alongside other therapies, so don't forget to ask your doctor about those too. And if you go ahead but find the side effects don't fade over time, talk to your doctor about the problems you're experiencing.

Summary

1. Medication for ADHD works well for some people, but there are side effects. Talk to your doctor about these before you start, and again if they become a problem.

2. Put reminders in place to prompt you to take your medication regularly.

3. Learn to know the "red flags" or warning signs for your medication and make sure family and friends are aware of them too.

Chapter 5: New Life, New Lifestyle

In the last chapter we looked at the kind of medication that's often prescribed for people with ADHD. Now let's take a look at other therapies that can help you. There are also things you can do to help yourself.

Medication is only useful for as long as you take the tablets. Of course it can be *very* helpful in controlling moods and behaviors, but in the long term it has a limited effect because it doesn't show you how to deal with the real issues. That's why it works best with other forms of therapy.

Choosing a therapist

People who see a therapist are taught to look at their problems in a different way. Normally used alongside medication, therapy aims to teach them how to begin controlling their ADHD symptoms for themselves.

This is often done by setting and achieving goals with a behavioral therapist. You could work on your relationships or timekeeping issues, for example. Or you might take a social skills class to learn to get on better with others. Some people find it helps to talk to a counselor about the way they feel. All these therapies are about finding ways to cope with your symptoms and improve your quality of life.

How do you go about finding a therapist or counselor? Well, the best way is to ask for around for a personal recommendation. You could try any of the following and ask them to recommend someone in your area who could help you with adult ADHD.

Your doctor

Your local hospital

Friends and family

Local non-profits and charities

Self-help groups and online forums

Once you start your therapy, try to be consistent. You will probably need to arrange for someone or something to remind you of your appointments, and maybe even to get you there on time! It's also a great idea to keep a diary or journal, as we mentioned earlier. It's a good way to see how much the therapy is helping.

So what now? Is there anything else that might help? Yep, there is.

A few simple changes

Many people with ADHD have found that making some very basic changes to their lifestyle can make a big difference. Together with medication and therapy, these simple ideas can be very powerful in controlling stress, which is a key factor for anyone with ADHD.

Sleep. Make sure you have enough sleep by getting into a regular pattern. Try to go to bed and get up at set times every day. Most people need seven to eight hours' sleep every night to give them focus and strength for the new day.

Exercise. We could all do with being more active, right? But for people with ADHD getting at least 30 minutes of exercise every day is especially important. It's a great way to get rid of some of that restlessness and de-stress at the same time.

Being out in the open while you exercise is best – walking the dog, hiking or running, for example – but indoors works too. Many people enjoy the challenging atmosphere of team sports or the discipline of martial arts. Pick something you enjoy and go for it!

Routines. Having a routine for everything is a great way to minimize stress. A calendar or wall chart in the kitchen is a practical way of organizing schedules and remembering routine events, like appointments with your therapist, for example.

It will also help you organize other regular events, like household tasks – putting the garbage out, or changing the sheets. Using different colored pens can be helpful too.

Many people with ADHD struggle to remember where they put things. As part of your routine-setting strategy, take time to decide on a place to keep your wallet, car keys and cellphone so you don't have to start each day hunting for them!

Write it down. Use a planner or organizer, or even a smartphone app, and note down everything. It's a great way to remember meetings, appointments and arrangements with others; you can include a to-do list as well to help you remember to buy the groceries or get the car fixed.

Diet. Try to aim for a healthy, balanced diet and avoid too many carbs and sugary foods. Some experts claim that plenty of Omega 3 can help with ADHD. Cut down on caffeine and alcohol – they both cause restless, edgy behaviors and can make you more impulsive and irritable.

Relaxation. We all know that this is a tricky area for anyone with ADHD, but it's important to find a way to unwind and de-stress. Not only will you function better, but your friends, family and co-workers will probably appreciate it if you're less tense and irritable!

When you need to relax at the end of the day and watching TV doesn't do it for you, you could try a quiet activity like listening to music, reading a good book, or even doing a crossword or jigsaw puzzle for an hour or two before bedtime (which are thought to help teach the brain to focus). This can help you feel relaxed and sleepy ready for bed, even if you thought you could keep going for hours yet. You could also try breathing exercises, meditation or yoga.

For days off and on weekends, why not find a new hobby? It's a great way to unwind. You might want to do something energetic, like walking a trail or taking up a sport. Maybe you're the social type and like to meet new people. What about martial arts, or even Latin dancing? Or maybe you'd prefer something creative, like writing or painting, or a handicraft of some kind. Whatever you choose, you need to relax just like everyone else.

Summary

1. Talk to your doctor about treatments like behavioral therapy. This can teach you to learn how to control some of your ADHD symptoms.

2. Simple lifestyle changes can make a big difference to someone with ADHD. These include changes to diet, setting regular hours for sleep and getting 30 minutes of exercise every day.

3. Minimize stress by structuring your life as much as possible. A calendar or wall chart can help you organize a routine and remember tasks and appointments.

4. Keep things clear in your mind by using an organizer or planner, or a smartphone app, and making notes and lists.

Chapter 6: ADHD in the Workplace

So far we've looked at medication, therapy and lifestyle changes that can all help someone with ADHD. Assuming you take all that on board, does it mean everything's going to be okay now?

Well, no. Not exactly.

All the things we've talked about so far are key factors in helping you get your symptoms under control, but let's be honest: someone with ADHD will probably still struggle with organization, concentration and memory. And it just happens that these are the areas that matter most in the workplace.

Many people with ADHD struggle at work. Some have lost their jobs; others have missed out on promotions or are stuck in low-paid positions, unable to advance because their lack of focus holds them back. In fact, almost half the adults with ADHD in the US are only holding down a part-time job.

Is there anything that can be done? Is it possible to be more organized at work? And the big question: should you come clean or try to keep your ADHD a secret?

Career choice

Some jobs are just not good for anyone with ADHD. Being restless and edgy doesn't make you an ideal candidate to operate delicate machinery or sell fragile ornaments, for example. Losing concentration or taking risks isn't a great recommendation for a banker, a lawyer or a school bus driver.

Build on your strengths and choose a career that suits your energy and the flow of new ideas you probably experience every day. Did you know that many people with ADHD are entrepreneurs? Setting up your own business also means you can set your own timetable.

If you don't feel you could do that, try to aim instead for something creative and fast-paced, without a rigid structure – maybe one that offers flexible hours. Talk to a career counselor about your strengths and weaknesses.

Improving productivity

So how are you going to keep this job once you've found it? Or any other job, for that matter! Well, even if you own the company you'll still be keen on making a profit, and your employer is no different. In this fast-paced world if you can't make the grade your boss will just find someone who can.

What can you do? Here are a few tips from webmd.com and psychcentral.com.

Distractions. You need to be able to focus, so try to keep distractions to a minimum. Ask if you can work in a quiet room instead of a cubicle or open-plan office. Wear headphones if necessary to cut out noise and hang up a "Please do not disturb" sign. Don't return voicemails and emails right away – set aside a time every day for doing that so you can keep your eye on the ball.

Planner. Use a planner and a to-do list. Add new items to the list and cross them off when done.

Notes. Take notes during phone calls and meetings – this helps you concentrate, gives you a release for your restless fingers and serves as a reminder later on. Add any tasks to your to-do list.

Timing. If you have several things you need to get done each day, block the time off for each one and set a timer on your phone or watch so you don't overrun. Keep to one thing at a time.

Meetings. Take notes to help keep you focused, or fiddle with your pen under the table. You may be able to move around quietly at the back of the room, or you could suggest everyone should feel free to get up and stretch their legs during long sessions.

Flexible working. What time of day are you most focused? Do your trickiest tasks then. Ask your boss if you can come in early or work late if that's what you need. Could you work from home, say once a week?

Release energy. Some people find it helps to have a bag of squishy balls or modeling clay in their drawer to fiddle with. Others choose an office chair that rocks. It's important to find a way to release your energy without disturbing other people.

Get help. You may be able to have an assistant to do the tasks you find most difficult – paperwork, for example. If you have a project to organize, work with a partner who can help you keep on track. Some people with ADHD find having someone working quietly next to them helps them stay focused.

Take a break. Take a short break every hour. Walk around outside, get a drink or have a quick chat and then get back to work. Relaxation techniques like breathing exercises can also help.

To speak or not to speak?

Is it better to tell your boss and co-workers about your ADHD, or keep quiet?

In the US, ADHD is classed as a disability. That means in theory your employer has to meet your needs. He also can't discriminate against you just because you have ADHD. Coming clean about your condition would give you the opportunity to explain about the way you work best. You should also point out your strengths: your energy, enthusiasm and creative ideas.

On the other hand, many experts advise against telling your boss about your condition. There are misconceptions and you could face prejudice, like having someone constantly looking for faults or micromanaging everything you do.

The website psychcentral.com gives these suggestions as a way of asking for help without spelling out why.

Too noisy to concentrate: "Is it possible to have a corner? I'm finding this level of noise very challenging."

Trouble with performance and setting goals: "Can we schedule a meeting today so I can understand our priorities?"

Afraid of missing details: "I work best if I take notes – is that OK?"

Too many meetings taking your time and focus: "Attending all these meetings isn't productive for me – can we look at which ones are the most critical?"

Summary

1. Choose a career that builds on your strengths, not your weaknesses. Talk to a career counselor for ideas.

2. Being upfront about your condition might let you explain yourself and what works best for you, but it can backfire and lead to prejudice.

3. Using planners and lists and setting a timer will help you get organized and keep on schedule. Take notes during meetings and phone calls. Return emails and voicemails at a set time to avoid breaking your concentration.

4. Build in breaks every hour and practice relaxation or breathing exercises to help you keep your focus.

Chapter 7: Relationships – It Takes Two

A key area for people with ADHD is relationships. There are almost always problems: fights, emotional outbursts and misunderstandings, angry scenes and even violence. And the person or people we often hurt are the ones we love most.

Good relationships are built on a basis of give and take: a partnership. Each party has a role to play, and gradually we come to trust the other person to play that role in the way we expect. This is true whether we're talking about a romantic involvement or a professional working relationship.

But for someone with ADHD they're all tricky. Poor concentration and memory, impulsive words or actions, restless energy, outbursts and irritability all add up. The result is often a trail of broken relationships, including divorce, and a lot of heartache.

What's really the problem here?

From our point of view, most of these relationship problems are made worse when one person has undiagnosed ADHD. This means that no one knows what's going wrong. The partnership has become unbalanced because the party with ADHD is struggling (or has given up trying) to meet the needs of the other person. And the person without ADHD has no idea why.

The website helpguide.org gives the example of a man who comes home from work to find his wife, who has undiagnosed ADHD, has failed to get dinner ready again. He complains about her bad timekeeping and unreliability, but really he sees it as a lack of care and consideration for him. "If she loved me she'd be sure I had a meal when I came home!"

She sees him as nagging and grumbling, not understanding the chores she has to get through with the kids and so on. "If he cared about me he wouldn't start up the moment he comes through the door! So I was a bit late – does that make me a bad wife?"

Sound familiar? There's more going on here than a late dinner. The couple's relationship is under stress as both have come to believe the other person no longer loves them.

So what can be done? Well, the first thing to do is to get that ADHD diagnosis. Find out for sure. Talk to a doctor, start a course of treatment and see a therapist – all the kinds of things we talked about earlier in the book.

Once you know, it's time to talk.

The ADHD love triangle

We've all heard of a love triangle, where a third party becomes romantically involved with someone who's already in a relationship. Well, it's the same here – only the third party is ADHD. Like it or not, ADHD is part of your relationships and it's a mistake to ignore it. And like all love triangles, there are some tough decisions ahead.

Okay, we're not suggesting you go round telling everyone you meet that you have ADHD and may have trouble fulfilling your side of the bargain! You don't even have to tell the people you work with or meet every day. That's up to you.

But in all fairness to you both you should tell the person you're romantically involved with, your "significant other." That way you can sit down and decide together how to make your partnership work.

Helpguide.org suggests you do it this way.

Put yourself in the other's shoes. Learn what life is like from their point of view.

Take it in turns to talk and listen. Avoid zoning out by taking notes and asking questions. If you lose focus, say so straight away and ask them to repeat it. If you can't stay calm, consider asking someone impartial to mediate.

Acknowledge the effect of your behavior. It takes two to tango! Admit that your partner has been suffering. It may come over as nagging, but in reality he or she is stressed out from carrying your share of the domestic chores and worries.

Take responsibility for your role. You played a part in causing the problems in your relationship; now you need to play a part in putting things right. Start by showing your partner you care about their feelings.

Working through the problems

Now you're both beginning to understand what's going on, you can find a way to rebalance your partnership, allowing for the problems that ADHD brings.

Divide. Analyze your strengths and weaknesses and divide the household chores between you. Maybe you'd be better at the cleaning and cooking while your non-ADHD partner takes care of bills and groceries, for example.

Evaluate. Schedule weekly appraisals to check how things are working. Are the chores split evenly? Is it working for you both? Is your relationship improving?

Finish. If you're having trouble getting things done, you could decide together as part of your agreement that your partner will finish off certain tasks while you take on something else.

Simplify. If you both feel things aren't working, try cutting the load by hiring a cleaner, getting your groceries delivered and paying bills automatically.

Organize a schedule. Work out a routine and stick to it to reduce stress and simplify things as much as possible. Use a memory board or planner, say in the kitchen. Keep clutter down by having a tidy house if you can – it helps minimize stress.

Summary

1. ADHD can make relationships difficult because of the forgetfulness, poor concentration, lack of organization and broken promises.

2. Talk through the problems with your partner and listen to their side of the story. Nagging and tears are often a sign of stress as your partner has been carrying most of the load. Let him or her know you care about them.

3. Work out a plan between you, focusing on your strengths. Use a wall chart in the kitchen to create a routine and divide the chores between you.

4. Evaluate the situation in a sit-down chat every week. If you need to, split tasks so your partner finishes what you start.

Simplify your domestic life by hiring a cleaner, getting your groceries delivered and paying bills automatically.

Chapter 8: More Tips and Strategies

So now we've looked at how ADHD can affect your working life and your home life. We've seen what you can do to improve these two areas. What else is there? Are there other strategies you can use to cope with this condition?

In this chapter we're going to take a look at a few other areas that can be tricky for someone with adult ADHD.

Strategies for handling money

Money is often a big problem for someone with both impulsivity and organizational issues. The website additudemag.com has some great suggestions to help you stay on budget.

Pay bills online. It takes a little time to set up, but paying bills online is ideal for people with ADHD as it's so much easier to manage. Arrange automatic payments for your regular bills then set aside a few hours every month to pay the rest online.

Track daily spending. Work out a weekly allowance for all non-essentials – a drink with friends, a pizza, a magazine or a movie... Take it out of the ATM on a set day (probably Friday, so you have it over the weekend) and keep it separate from your household budget. That money has to last you all week, and a quick glance in your wallet tells you whether you can afford any treats.

Freeze your credit card. Have one strictly for emergencies – but keep it in a block of ice in the freezer so you're not tempted to use it unless you really have to.

Save receipts. Only keep receipts if you need to show proof of purchase or claim tax-deductible expenses. Put these receipts straight into a hanging wall pocket in your kitchen or breakfast room. At the end of the month transfer them to a large envelope, write the month and year on the front and seal it. Keep it with your tax documents.

File for tax documents. Keep all your tax documentation for the year in a special wallet or file. A plastic one with a handle makes it waterproof and highly portable. Any tax documentation that arrives in the mail can go straight into this file and won't get lost in a pile of paperwork.

Strategies for timekeeping

This is one of the key problem areas for people with ADHD. Fortunately, there are plenty of useful apps for your computer and smartphone to help you plan, organize and keep track of time. Here are a few more ideas from additudemag.com.

Use a flying alarm clock. If you have trouble getting out of bed, try a flying alarm clock. Almost impossible to ignore, you have to get up fast to catch it before it crashes.

Time yourself. People with ADHD often underestimate how long a task will take. Use a stopwatch to time your regular journeys or daily chores so you can plan more accurately.

Allow extra time. Don't plan to arrive anywhere right on time, because you'll be late! Plan to arrive 15 or even 30 minutes early. You can always catch up on your reading or paperwork while you're waiting.

Set two alarms, not one. Each time you have to leave off doing something to go out, set two alarms on your watch or cellphone, five minutes apart. When the first goes off, grab your stuff and go. Be out of the house or office before the second alarm sounds.

Don't stop for distractions. Some people find it helps to repeat out loud what they're supposed to be doing to avoid getting distracted. For example, if you're leaving for work keep saying to yourself "I'm going to the car, I'm going to the car." That way you're less likely to stop and do something else.

Tips for beating stress

It can be pretty stressful to feel you're constantly struggling to cope with a mountain of tasks while surrounded by piles of paperwork and things you haven't got round to doing yet.

In this book we've laid out different strategies and suggestions to help you get a little more organization in your life. But it will take time to teach yourself new habits, so how can you cope with stress in the meantime?

Declutter and tidy away. Reduce the sense of stress by having things out of sight in cupboards, on shelves or in boxes under beds as much as possible. Have a home filing system that works. If you have nowhere to put things away, buy a sideboard or shelving unit. Get rid of things you don't need and give yourself a relaxing environment without clutter.

Plan for the next day. Write out a plan for tomorrow before you go to bed. It helps get your thoughts in order so you awake more refreshed and already focused.

Relax. Learn some breathing exercises, practice yoga or meditation or listen to soft music to help you unwind. Alternatively, make time to go for a run, meet up with friends or take up a hobby or sport.

Ask for help. You might consider hiring a professional ADHD coach to help you get organized. Failing that, don't keep things bottled up – talk to someone and ask for advice. Try some of the ADHD forums and chat rooms to get suggestions from others in the same situation as you.

Don't get obsessed. It may surprise you, but some people with ADHD end up with obsessive-compulsive disorder because they've become over-concerned with order and method. If this sounds like you, talk to your doctor or therapist, or see a counselor to discuss better coping strategies.

Summary

1. Try out a few simple strategies to help you handle finance and timekeeping issues. Find which ones work for you.

2. Manage your stress levels by learning relaxation exercises and planning ways to unwind and have fun. Let off steam by chatting with others on ADHD forums.

3. Consider hiring an ADHD coach to help you get organized. If you find you're becoming obsessed with organization, speak to your doctor or a counselor to avoid developing obsessive-compulsive disorder.

Conclusion

This book has given you information and strategies for helping you cope with ADHD. If you've got to this point, congratulations! You're now better equipped to understand your condition and find ways to help you deal with it.

Let's just summarize the key points we made.

1. Diagnosis. If you're concerned about your ability to focus and your personal organization, you may have ADHD. See a doctor!

2. Treatment. Once you know for sure, ask about the therapies available. Start a course of medication, if that's recommended. See a therapist to start learning new skills and strategies. Remember, several therapies are more effective than just one.

3. Lifestyle changes. Bring structure to your life by setting up routines. Use a planner or wall chart to help you do this. Block in regular times for sleeping, eating and exercising, and regular chores like paying bills or putting out the garbage.

4. Coping strategies. Get into the habit of writing everything down. Use a planner or organizer and make to-do lists. Take notes during discussions and phone calls. Time yourself and set alarms on your watch or cellphone so you don't spend too long on one task.

5. Relationships. ADHD puts a strain on your relationships. Acknowledge that your partner's nagging or scolding is largely due to stress because they've been left to cope. Sit down together and work out a strategy for sharing the load based on your strengths and weaknesses.

6. Relaxation. Stress is bad for anyone, and people with ADHD find it especially tough. Build in mini-breaks every hour at work so you can maintain focus. Find ways to relax and unwind at home by taking up a hobby or sport. Make sure you have someone to share the load with – maybe via an ADHD chat room.

By putting these strategies in place you can start to win your struggle with ADHD. And remember, you're not on your own. Take a look at some of the great ADHD websites like additudemag.com and CHADD. There are plenty more, and you may also find a support group in your area.

If there's nothing where you live, why not consider starting one yourself? Don't let ADHD slow you down. You have the energy and ideas to make a great difference to others, so why not give it a try?

CPSIA information can be obtained at www.ICGtesting.com
Printed in the USA
LVOW10s0644080716

495498LV00034B/831/P